ANIMAL KINGDOM
BEARS

Written by Alex Hall

American adaptation copyright © 2026 by North Star Editions, Mendota Heights, MN 55120. All rights reserved. No part of this book may be reproduced or utilized in any form or by any means without written permission from the publisher.

Bears © 2024 BookLife Publishing
This edition is published by arrangement with BookLife Publishing

sales@northstareditions.com | 888-417-0195

Library of Congress Control Number:
2024952953

ISBN
978-1-952455-30-8 (library bound)
978-1-952455-86-5 (paperback)
978-1-952455-67-4 (epub)
978-1-952455-50-6 (hosted ebook)

Printed in the United States of America
Mankato, MN
092025

Written by:
Alex Hall

Edited by:
Elise Carraway

Designed by:
Ker Ker Lee

All facts, statistics, web addresses and URLs in this book were verified as valid and accurate at time of writing. No responsibility for any changes to external websites or references can be accepted by either the author or publisher.

Photo Credits – Images courtesy of Shutterstock.com, unless otherwise stated.

Cover – Eric Isselee, Anan Kaewkhammul, Rosa Jay, unive, Martin Mecnarowski, Anan Kaewkhammul, zeelbervarg, photomaster, Hung Chung Chih, Adilson Sochodolak, Chase D'animulls, MR.Silaphop Pongsa. 4–5 – apple2499, RilakkuMaxx, Chase D'animulls, stativius. 6–7 – notsuperstar, NCDomingo. 8–9 – Dennis van de Water, Bbu Kurkovva, Anan Kaewkhammul. 10–11 – Christian Musat, WildMedia, Alexey Seafarer, zeelbervarg. 12–13 – DINESH DUGGIRALA, Martin Mecnarowski, Ondrej Prosicky. 14–15 – BlueBarronPhoto, unive, ducu59us, Svetlana Foote. 16–17 – Eric Isselee, Matyas Rehak, Kai T, xpixel, aleksander hunta. 18–19 – Eric Isselee, NaturesMomentsuk, Alexey Seafarer. 20–21 – Mark A. McCaffrey, nwdph, Dennis W Donohue, Giedriius. 22–23 – Luis Molinero, evaurban, Eric Isselee, Stanley Kalvan, ermess.

CONTENTS

Page 4	Bears
Page 6	Body of a Bear
Page 8	Types of Bears
Page 10	Habitats
Page 12	Amazing Bear Abilities
Page 14	Helpful Bears
Page 16	Diet
Page 18	Life Cycle of a Polar Bear
Page 20	Believe It or Not!
Page 22	Are You a Genius Kid?
Page 24	Glossary and Index

Words that look like this can be found in the glossary on page 24.

BEARS

Bears come in different sizes and colors. They live all around the world. What types of bears do you know? What do they look like?

Do they have tiny ears and sharp teeth? Maybe they have big paws and black noses.

Bears are mammals. Mammals are warm-blooded animals that have a backbone and make milk to feed their young.

All bears are part of a group called the Ursidae <u>family</u>.

DID YOU KNOW?
An animal with a backbone is called a vertebrate.

BODY OF A BEAR

From black bears to panda bears, all bears have these main body parts.

NOSE

Bears use their noses to find food, sense danger, and <u>communicate</u> with other bears.

DID YOU KNOW?

Polar bears have the strongest sense of smell of all bears.

FUR

Many bears have fur to help keep them warm. Some bears' fur protects their skin from rain and sunshine.

PAWS

All bears have large, wide feet. They have five toes and sharp claws. Different bears use their feet for different jobs.

CLAWS

Many bears use their claws to dig, hold food, and climb trees.

TYPES OF BEARS

There are eight different types of bears. Here are a few of them:

There are more North American black bears than any other type of bear. They have short claws that help them climb trees. North American black bears usually live alone.

Pandas are black and white bears. They have a false thumb made from their wrist bone. It helps them hold bamboo.

Sun bears are known for the golden marking on their chest. It looks like a sunrise.

DID YOU KNOW?
Sun bears are often known as honey bears.

HABITATS

Habitats are the natural homes in which animals, plants, and other living things live. Habitats have everything the living things need, including food, water, and shelter.

Some bears live in warm habitats.

Andean bears live in warm South American mountains. Andean bears are also called spectacled bears.

Most bears live in <u>mild</u> or cold habitats.

Polar bears live on snow and ice in the freezing cold Arctic.

Brown bears live in woodlands and meadows. North American brown bears are often known as grizzly bears.

AMAZING BEAR ABILITIES

Bears have many adaptations to help them live in their habitats.

SLURP IT UP
Sloth bears can suck insects out of their nests. They wrap their lower lip around the edge of their nose. Then, they pull the insects through a toothless gap in their mouth.

NAPTIME IS ANYTIME
Some sloth bears sleep during the day, and others sleep at night.

BRAINY BEARS
Many bears know how to use tools. Polar bears are known to hunt walruses by dropping rocks on them.

13

HELPFUL BEARS

Bears can be helpful to the natural world.

FISHY FARMING
Many bears catch fish to eat. Sometimes, they drag the fish across the forest floor. The bodies of the fish leave <u>nutrients</u> in the soil. These nutrients help more plants grow.

STINKY SEEDING

Some bears eat fruit and plants. The seeds come out in their poop. Bears poop in many different areas. This helps the seeds to spread so more plants can grow.

BEAR BALANCE

The natural world needs balance. Bears eat many different plants. This helps keep plant life balanced.

DIET

A diet is the food a person or animal usually eats. Different types of bears have different diets.

Polar bears are carnivores. Carnivores are animals that eat other animals. Polar bears often eat seals or fish.

Pandas are mostly herbivores. Herbivores eat plants. Pandas mainly eat bamboo. However, they sometimes eat fish and small mammals.

DID YOU KNOW?
Pandas spend around 12 hours eating bamboo every day.

Most bears are omnivores. Omnivores eat plants and other animals.

17

LIFE CYCLE OF A POLAR BEAR

As a bear grows, it goes through several changes. Each change is part of a stage. Together, these stages make up the bear's life cycle.

CUB

Young polar bears are called cubs. Cubs are born inside snow dens. They stay in the dens for around four months.

ADOLESCENT
Older cubs learn to hunt. They stay with their mother for around two years.

ADULT
Polar bears become adults at around three to five years old. They have their own young to continue the life cycle.

DID YOU KNOW?
Polar bears usually live for 20 to 30 years.

BELIEVE IT OR NOT!

Polar bears and Kodiak brown bears are the world's largest land carnivores.

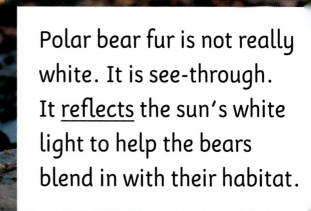

Polar bear fur is not really white. It is see-through. It <u>reflects</u> the sun's white light to help the bears blend in with their habitat.

Not all black bears are black. Some have light brown fur to blend in with their habitat. Their lighter fur helps them to stay cool in warmer habitats.

Bears have good memories. They can remember the places where they found food years ago.

ARE YOU A GENIUS KID?

You now know a lot about bears. Let's test your knowledge to see how much you really know! Are you really a genius kid?

Check back through the book if you are not sure.

1. What are Andean bears also known as?

2. How do bears spread fruit seeds?

3. Why do some black bears have brown-colored fur?

Answers: 1. Spectacled bears, 2. They spread seeds through their poop, 3. It helps them blend into their surroundings and stay cool

GLOSSARY

adaptations changes to animals that have happened over time to help them be better suited to their environment

communicate to pass information between two or more living things

family a way of grouping animals with very similar traits

mild not extreme

nutrients natural substances that plants and animals need to grow

reflects bounces back light, heat, or sound

INDEX

claws 7–8
fish 14, 16–17
food 6–7, 10, 16, 21
forests 14
fur 7, 20–21, 23

meadows 11
mountains 10
paws 4, 7
seeds 15, 23
trees 7, 8